Autism & PDD™
Social Skills Lessons

Pam Britton Reese
Nena C. Challenner

Skill Areas: Social Skills/Language
Ages: 3 thru 8

LinguiSystems

LinguiSystems, Inc.
3100 4th Avenue
East Moline, IL 61244-9700
1-800 PRO IDEA
1-800-776-4332

FAX: 1-800-577-4555
E-mail: service@linguisystems.com
Web: www.linguisystems.com
TDD: 1-800-933-8331
          (for those with hearing impairments)

Printed in the U.S.A.

ISBN 0-7606-0298-0

About the Authors

Pam Britton Reese, M.A., CCC-SLP, owns a private practice, CommunicAid Plus, where she provides speech and language services to children and adults. She is also an educational consultant to public and private schools. Pam has over 9 years experience in the schools as a speech-language pathologist and teacher of the hearing-impaired. She has worked with young children with autism and PDD since 1995. *Autism & PDD: Social Skills Lessons* is her first publication with LinguiSystems.

Nena C. Challenner, B.S., is a PPCD (Preschool Program for Children with Disabilities) Instructor and Inclusion Specialist. She has been a teacher for over 15 years and has taught preschool through second grade. She has worked with children with autism and PDD since 1995. *Autism & PDD: Social Skills Lessons* is her first publication with LinguiSystems.

Acknowledgments

Thanks to my husband, Joe, for his support and enthusiasm, and to my children, Kate, Matthew, and Sam for their patience and understanding – PBR

Thanks to my parents, Glen A. Zachary and Betty Y. Zachary, for their love and encouragement that will be with me always, and to my husband, Phillip, and my son, Ryan, for their patience and support throughout the writing of this book – NCC

And thanks to Amy Ballard for sharing her artistic ability on our very first social lesson, to Julie Nelson for sharing her wide expertise on children's behavior, and to Judy Walling, Special Education Director, Midlothian ISD, for expanding the world of children with special needs.

Dedication

To Shawn, for showing us a way to teach children with autism

Illustrations by Eulala Conner
Page Layout by Christine Buysse

Table of Contents

Introduction

A few years ago, we were working together to facilitate the inclusion of a five-year-old boy with autism into a kindergarten/first-grade classroom. Communication with the child was a problem. Although the classroom had been structured to aid his inclusion, inappropriate behaviors repeatedly set him back both academically and socially. Some of his typical behaviors were climbing on desktops, darting, squirting glue on tables, dumping toys, and pulling on electrical cords.

We learned of Carol Gray's success with stories describing social situations to teach children with autism. The format of Gray's stories in *The New Social Story Book* (1994) seemed perfect for our student. However, due to the child's young age, we soon found that those stories were too long. Shorter sentences and stories plus the addition of pictures were critical to his comprehension. So we began writing one-page lessons with each sentence supported by one or more pictures. Our lessons targeted typical needs of preschool and early primary students.

Our lessons were so successful that we began using them with other children with autism and PDD. As parents began to see how the lessons worked at school, they requested lessons concerning behaviors at home and in the community. In addition, the lessons were used successfully with children with other disabilities and with typically-developing children. *Autism & PDD: Social Skills Lessons* is the culmination of the work we did with teachers and families over the last few years.

About the Books

The lessons are grouped into five separate books:

- School
- Home
- Community
- Getting Along
- Behavior

In each book, we have included two types of lessons: instructional and behavioral. The instructional lessons are intended to teach young children what they need to do or say in social situations that are often overwhelming to children with autism (e.g., *Receiving a Compliment*, Getting Along book, page 13). The instructional lessons can be used as part of a social skills curriculum with small groups of children or individuals. The behavioral lessons target specific social problems that need to be stopped. They are best used with an individual child (e.g., *Running Away (Darting)*, Behavior book, page 27).

The lessons are not intended to be used in the order presented, but chosen according to the needs of a particular child.

Educators have had success using social skills lessons at school, and the lessons are equally as effective at home. The lessons included in the *Home* book were written with input from families of children with autism. Their experiences with the lessons taught us some things to consider when using the lessons at home.

- Target only one or two behaviors at a time.

Introduction, *continued*

- When possible, post the lesson in the room where the behavior occurs. For example, *Brushing Teeth* can be posted in the bathroom near the sink.

- Many children benefit from having a copy of the lesson to hold and review on their own.

- Don't worry if a child needs the lesson read over several days before seeing a change in the behavior.

- Once the behavior fades, it is not necessary to read the lesson on a daily basis. However, should the behavior reoccur, the lesson should be read again with the child.

Make the Lessons Fit the Child

No two children are the same! Although the lessons are ready for use as they appear in the books, it will undoubtedly be necessary to make changes in some lessons to fit the child. For example, some children may not understand that the generic child used in the lessons refers to them. For these children, attach a photograph of the child in the upper right-hand corner of the lesson. As you read the story, point to the photograph and say the child's name in place of any pronouns. Continue to use the lesson as written. In time, some children may learn to accept the use of the generic child.

Editing may also be needed if the chosen lesson does not exactly match what the child is doing. For example, in the *Squirting Glue* lesson (Behavior book, page 15), we show the child squirting glue on tables. If the child is squirting glue on the floor or on other children, you will need to change the lesson. Cross out the text and rewrite the sentence following the format of the original sentence.

Blank lines have been inserted in the text in some lessons to help you individualize them for each child. There are empty spaces above the lines for additional pictures if needed. The picture index in the back of each book contains pictures that may be copied and substituted. If you can't find the picture you need in the index, feel free to substitute or add photographs, your own line drawings, copies of pictures from another lesson in one of the other books, *Boardmaker* Software (1995), or other computer-generated clip art.

Using the Lessons

Identify the skill to be taught. No child will need every lesson. Search for the source of the problem. Is it sensory? Is it a communication breakdown? Is the child sick? Some problems can be solved by ignoring the behavior or changing something in the environment. Limit the number of lessons presented at one time. Start with one or two. Wait until they are learned before introducing more.

Choose the appropriate lesson and make two copies. Change the story as needed. Place one copy of the lesson in a notebook for the child. As skills are presented and learned, the notebook can be used for reviewing lessons with the child and for sharing the lessons with other teachers, parents, and caregivers. The second copy is to be used for direct instruction with the child as follows:

1. Identify the time and place the social situation occurs. The *Tracking Multiple Behaviors* form, page 50, and/or the *Initial Behavior Analysis* form, page 52, will help you.

Introduction, *continued*

2. When teaching a new skill, the social lesson should immediately precede the targeted situation. For example, if the child is having a problem completing seatwork, read *I Finish My Work* (School book, page 14) just before you hand out the work.

3. Present the lesson. Sit with the child one-on-one in a quiet area and read the lesson aloud. Point to the pictures for emphasis. Read the lesson again.

4. Allow the child to keep the lesson. This allows the child to review the lesson repeatedly as the new skill is learned. Don't worry if this copy is damaged or discarded by the child since you have another copy in the child's notebook.

5. Document the lesson(s) taught using the *Record of Progress*, page 54, and/or the tracking forms on pages 56-59. These records can serve as documentation for IEP objectives and behavioral intervention.

Special Considerations

Pronouns can be difficult for some children with autism. We have used "I" extensively throughout the books as a way to help teach the pronoun. If pronoun use prevents comprehension of the lesson, substitute the child's name in the text and/or use the child's photograph in place of the "I" symbol.

Be sure to use words that the child is familiar with (e.g., gym vs. P.E.; jungle gym vs. monkey bars).

The lesson and pictures on one page may be overwhelming for some children. You can use a blank sheet of paper to mask the rest of the lesson as you read each line. The lessons can also be used to make a small book. Cut apart the sentences and accompanying pictures. Place each sentence/pictures in the center of a separate sheet of paper. Staple the pages together to make a book.

These lessons can easily be adapted to the child's language and comprehension level. If necessary, delete words to shorten sentences. Some children may also need fewer pictures per sentence. We have even used lessons with no text for behavior (e.g., bite/time-out) and instruction (e.g., work/computer).

Adult: "If I bite (point), time out (point)."

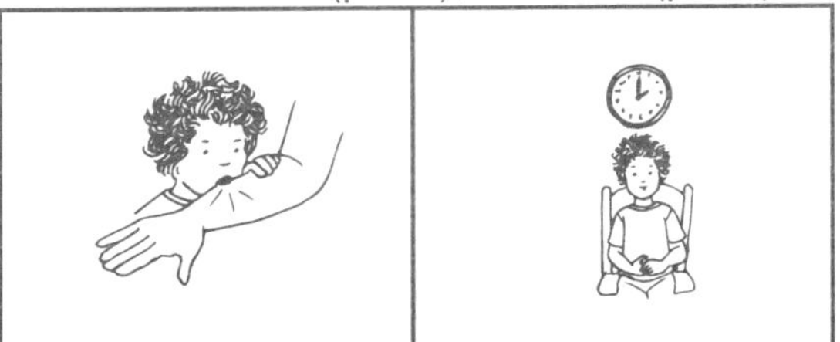

Adult: "If I finish work (point), computer (point)."

These lessons do not offer a solution to the myriad of challenges presented by young children with autism and PDD. They have, however, proved to be a useful tool for many families, teachers, and speech-language pathologists to teach children with autism and PDD to understand the social world in which they live. We hope that you will find these social skills lessons as effective as we have.

Pam and Nena

Morning Routine

In the morning I get out of bed.

_______________ cooks breakfast.
(person)

I use the toilet.

I wash my face and hands.

I put on my clothes.

_______________ says, "Time to eat breakfast."*
(person)

*Draw in clock hands to show the appropriate time.

Getting Dressed

I can put on my clothes.

First I take off my pajamas.

________________ helps me choose my clothes.
(person)

I put on shirt, pants, socks, and shoes.

I try to do it by myself.

I can ask for help.

Wearing Different Clothes

I like to wear my ________________.
(piece of clothing)

I can wear my ________________ one day.
(piece of clothing)

Then I take off my ________________.
(piece of clothing)

________________ will wash my ________________.
(person)   (piece of clothing)

Now I can wear my ________________ again.
(piece of clothing)

Mealtime: I Eat My Own Food

I eat with my family.

I have a plate. _________________ has a plate.

(person)

I eat the food on my plate.

I do not eat the food on _________________'s plate.

(person)

I eat my own food. _________________ is happy.

(person)

Trying New Food

I like to eat _______________.
(favorite food)

_______________ says, "Try a bite of _______________."
(person) (new food)

I can do it.

I have a bite of _______________.
(new food)

_______________ is happy.
(person)

Going to Bed

I go to bed at ________________.
(time*)

________________ says, "Time to go to bed."*
(person)

Sometimes I get a drink of water.

Sometimes I listen to a story.

I hug and say, "Good night."

I go to sleep.

*Draw in clock hands to show the appropriate time.

Weekend Morning

I wake up.

I get out of bed and say, "Good morning."

If ________________ is sleeping, I can play with toys.
  (person)

I can look at a book.

I can watch cartoons.

________________ is happy when I am quiet.
  (person)

Cleaning My Room

Toys are on the floor in my room.

________________ says, "Time to clean up."
(person)

I put clothes in the basket.

I put toys in the toy box.

I help ________________.
(person)

I clean up my room.  ________________ is happy.
(person)

After-school Day-care

I go to day-care after school. It is okay.

Sometimes I play with friends.

Sometimes I color and draw.

Sometimes I have a snack.

_________________________ will come to pick me up at _______________________.
(person)   (time*)

*Draw in clock hands to show the appropriate time.

Brushing Teeth

I brush my teeth.

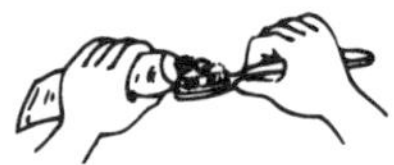

I put a little toothpaste on the toothbrush.

I brush and brush and brush.

I spit in the sink.

I swish water in my mouth and spit it out.

Finished!

Shampooing Hair

My hair is dirty. ________________ washes my hair.
(person)

My hair gets wet.

________________ rubs my hair with shampoo.
(person)

My hair gets wet again.

I am finished. ________________ helps me dry my hair.
(person)

Clipping Fingernails

My fingernails are too long.

_________________ trims them for me.
(person)

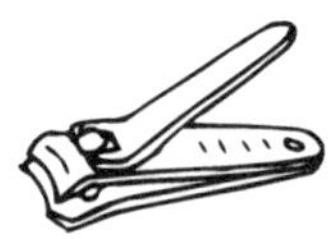

We use special clippers.

I stick out a finger. The clippers go "Snip, snip."

It is okay.

_________________ clips all my fingernails.
(person)

Bath Time

_______________ says, "Time to take a bath!"
(person)

I take off my clothes.

I use the toilet.

I sit in the water. It feels good!

Sometimes I play with toys.

_______________ helps me wash with soap.
(person)

Using the Toilet

I sit on the toilet. _________________ sets the timer.
(person)

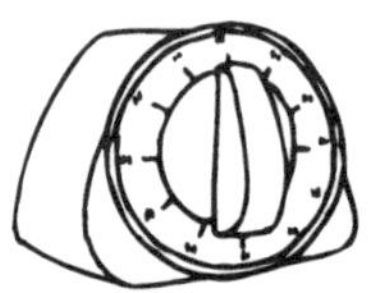

My _________________ goes in the toilet.
(tee-tee/poop*)

The timer goes "Ding."

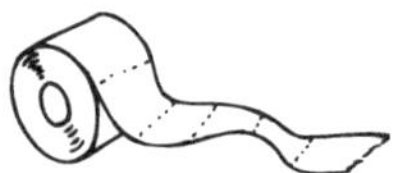

I wipe myself with toilet paper.

I flush the toilet.

I am finished. I wash my hands.

*Substitute any word the child is familiar with.

Taking Medicine

I need medicine.

_________________ gives me medicine.
(person)

I swallow my medicine.

The medicine tastes like _______________.
(flavor)

_________________ is happy when I take my medicine.
(person)

Answering Machine

A light blinks on the answering machine.

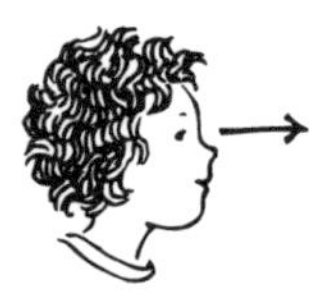

I can look at the light.

The answering machine has buttons.

I do not touch the buttons. This is important.

_______________________ will use the answering machine.
(person)

The Vacuum Cleaner

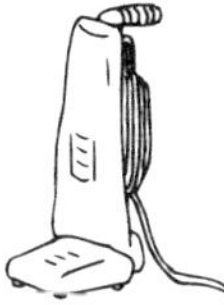 

The vacuum cleaner makes a loud noise.

I can cover my ears. It is okay.

I can go to a different room.

The vacuum cleaner sucks up dirt.

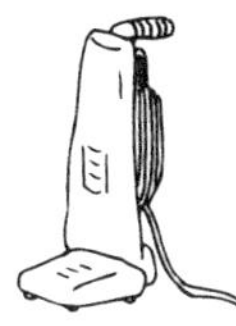 

The vacuum cleaner will stop soon.

Electrical Outlets

_______________ plugs things in.
(person)

The plug goes in the holes.

This makes things go.

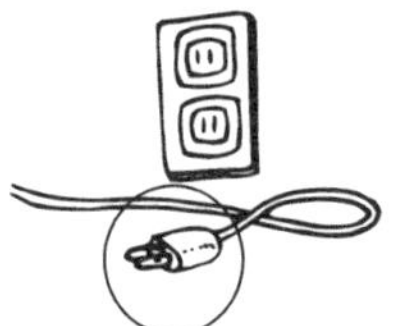 

Only plugs go in holes. This is important.

Only _______________ plugs things in.
(person)

Hot and Cold Water

H means hot water.

C means cold water.

I only use cold water.

_______________________ helps me with hot water.
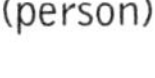
(person)

 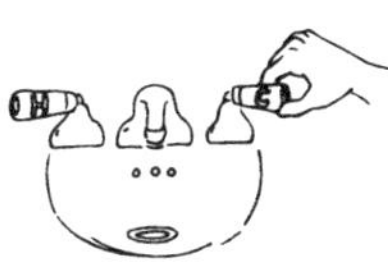

I only use cold water.

Hot Iron

_________________ uses an iron on clothes.
(person)

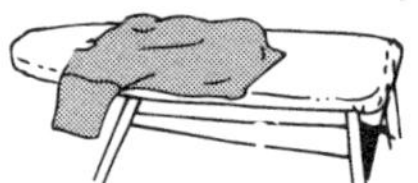

The clothes go on the ironing board.

The iron is very hot.

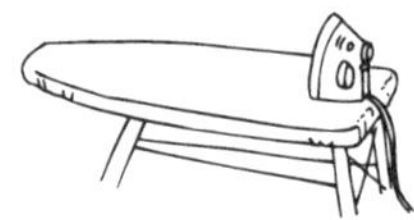 

The iron stays on the ironing board. This is important.

Only_________________ uses the iron.
(person)

Hot Stove

_______________ cooks food on the stove.
(person)

The stove is hot.

I do not touch the stove. This is important.

I do not touch pot handles.

I stand far from the stove.

The Microwave

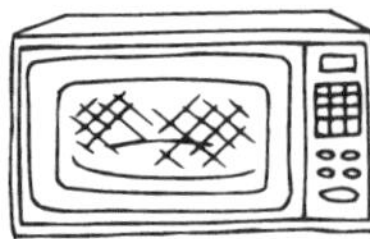

_______________ uses the microwave.
(person)

Only food goes in the microwave.

The microwave cooks food.

I do not touch the buttons.

I watch _______________ use the microwave.
(person)

Wearing My Seat Belt

I put on my seat belt in the car.

I do not take my seat belt off. This is important.

I stay in my seat with my seat belt on.

I can look out the window.

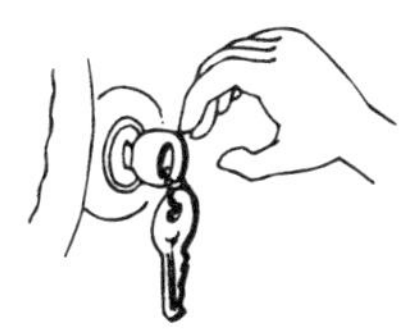

_________________ turns the car off.
(person)

I can take off my seat belt now.

Sitting in the Back Seat

I sit in the back seat.

This is important.

______________________ can sit in the front seat.
(adult)

It is okay. I am safe in the back seat.

______________________ is happy when I sit in the back seat.

Getting Help

Sometimes I need help.

I can go to ________________.
(person)

I will say, "Help me, please."

I will ask for help quietly.

________________ is happy when I ask for help.
(person)

Others Talking on the Phone

When _________ talks on the phone, I cannot talk to _________.
    (person)   (person)

When _________ talks on the phone, I cannot stand by _________.
    (person)   (person)

I can play on the computer.

I can watch TV.

I can do my dot-to-dot.

I cannot talk to or stand by ______ when ______ talks on the phone.
                                     (person)   (person)

Favorite TV Show

________________ comes on at ________________ .
(favorite TV show)   (time*)

I watch it for 30 minutes.

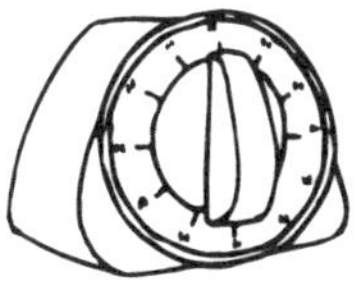

________________ sets the timer.
(person)

When the timer goes "Ding," ________________ is over.
(name of TV show)

It is okay. ________________ will come on again.
(name of TV show)

*   Draw in clock hands to show appropriate time.

Watching One TV

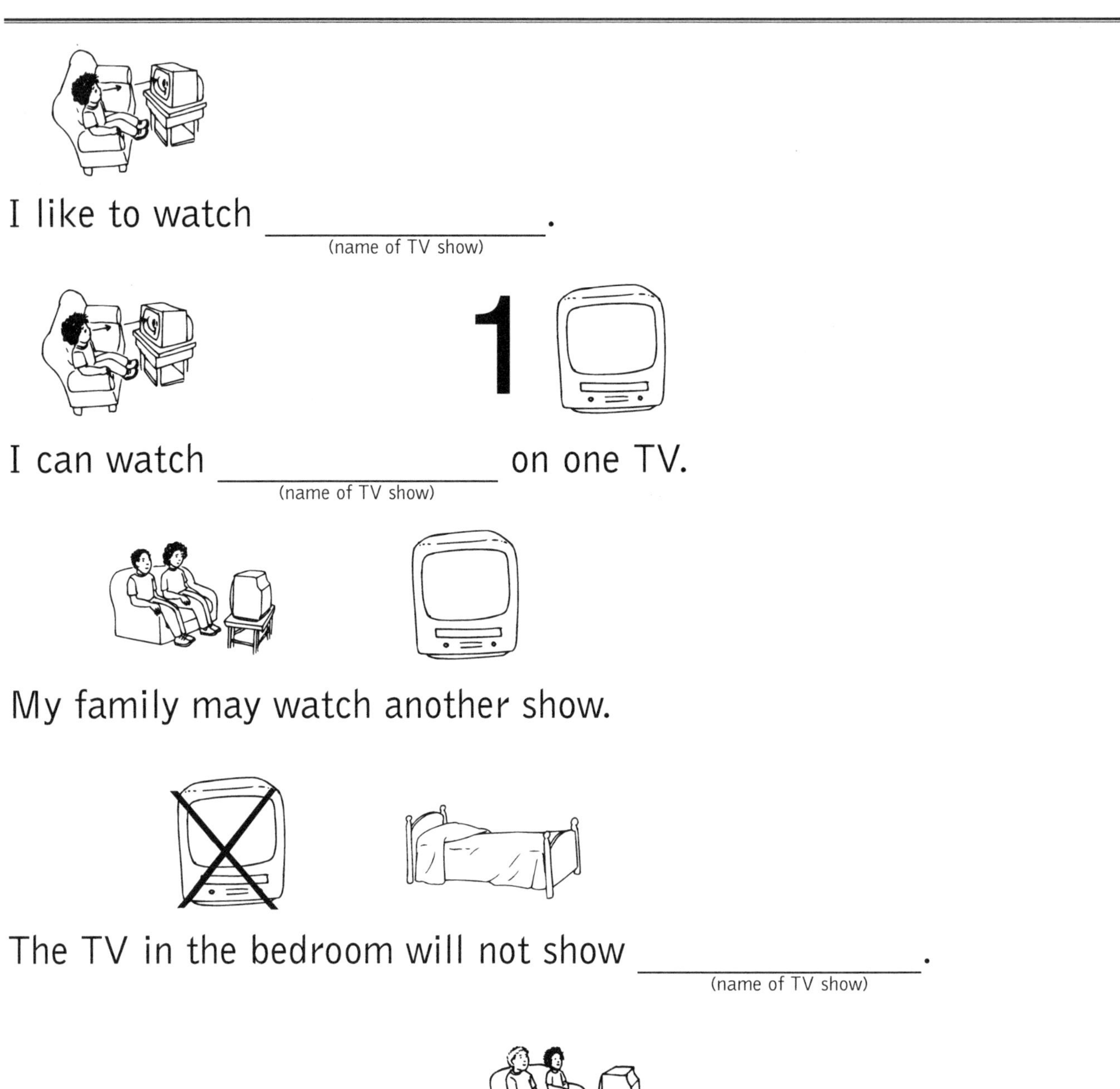

I like to watch ______________.
(name of TV show)

I can watch ______________ on one TV.
(name of TV show)

My family may watch another show.

The TV in the bedroom will not show ______________.
(name of TV show)

Sometimes ______________ will watch ______________ with me.
(person)   (name of TV show)

Sharing the TV

I can choose a show on TV.

_______________ can watch it too.
(person)

When my show is finished, _______________ can choose a show.
(person)

I can watch TV with _______________.
(person)

It is okay. We can watch TV together.

Sharing the Computer

I like to use the computer.

________________ can use the computer too.
(person)

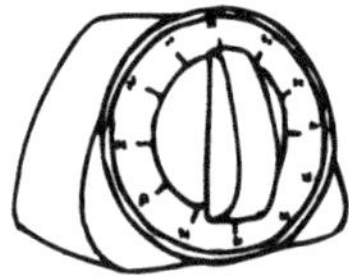

________________ will set the timer.
(person)

The timer goes "Ding."   My turn is over.

The timer goes "Ding" again.   It is my turn.

Pets

I like my pet.

I am gentle with my pet.

I feed my pet when _______________ tells me.
(person)

I give my pet water.

I take care of my pet.

People Go Away

________________ goes away in the car.
(person)

It is okay. ________________ will come back.
(person)

A baby-sitter stays with me.

The baby-sitter will take care of me.

________________ will come back soon.*
(person)

* Draw in clock hands to show appropriate time.

The Baby-sitter

A baby-sitter stays with me.

The baby-sitter says, "Time to eat." I sit down and eat.

The baby-sitter says, "Time to take a bath." I take a bath.

The baby-sitter says, "Time to go to bed." I get in my bed.

I am nice to the baby-sitter.

______________ will come back. ______________ will be happy.
(person)　　　　　　　　　　　　　　(person)

Not Going on a Trip

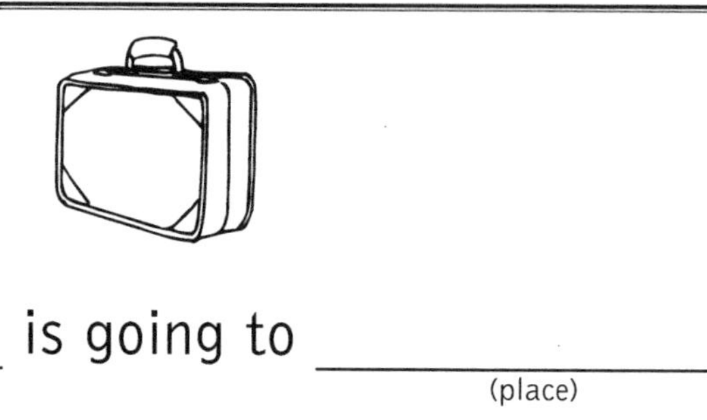

_________________ is going to _________________.
(person)   (place)

_________________ will stay in _____________ for _____________ days.*
(person)   (place)   (number)

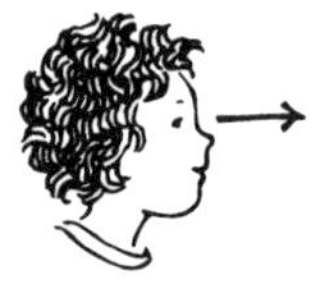 

I look at my calendar.

I make an X on each day.

   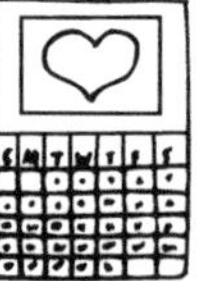

_________________ will come home after _______________ days.*
(person)   (number)

*Circle the number of days the adult will be away.

Staying Away from Home

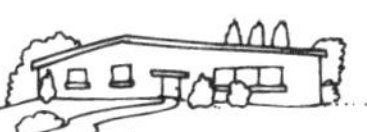

I stay at ________________'s house.
(person)

I eat food.

I take a bath.

I sleep in a bed.

I am nice to ________________.
(person)

I will go home on ________________.*

*Circle the day the child will go home.

Time-out

Sometimes _____________ is upset.
(person)

I go to time-out.

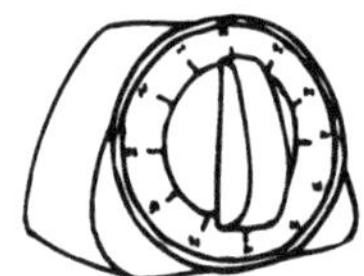

_____________ sets the timer.
(person)

I sit quietly.

The timer goes "Ding." Time-out is finished.

It is okay. _____________ loves me.
(person)

Sick Sibling Stays Home

_______________ is sick and stays at home.
(person)

_______________ stays at home with _______________.
(person)   (person)

I am not sick.

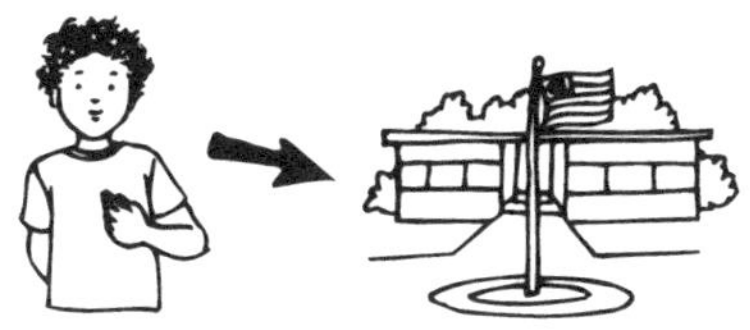

I go to school.

My teacher and friends are at school.

Having Company

Friends are coming to my house.

________________ talks to friends.
(person)

I do not interrupt. This is important.

It is my turn. I can talk to friends.

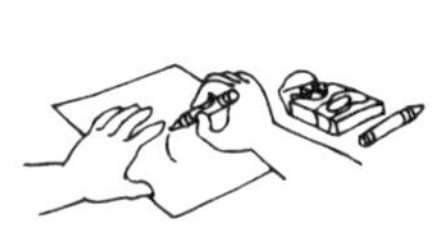

I can color while friends talk.

I am nice to friends.

My Birthday

Today is my birthday. I am _______________ years old.
(number)

Friends sing "Happy Birthday."

I blow out candles on my cake.

I eat cake with friends.

I open presents.

I say "Thank you" to friends.

The Sprinkler

In summer, it is hot.

The sprinkler puts water on the grass.

________________ tells me when I can run in the sprinkler.
(person)

The water sprays on me. It is okay.

It is cold. It feels good.

It is fun to run in the sprinkler.

Picture Index

People

Things

Houses

Tracking Multiple Behaviors

Child's Name _______________________________   Date _______________________________

Behavior	Behavior	Behavior	Behavior	Behavior
Time 1 / Location	Time 1 / Location	Time 1 / Location	Time 1 / Location	Time 1 / Location
Antecedent	Antecedent	Antecedent	Antecedent	Antecedent
Consequence	Consequence	Consequence	Consequence	Consequence
Time 2 / Location	Time 2 / Location	Time 2 / Location	Time 2 / Location	Time 2 / Location
Antecedent	Antecedent	Antecedent	Antecedent	Antecedent
Consequence	Consequence	Consequence	Consequence	Consequence
Time 3 / Location	Time 3 / Location	Time 3 / Location	Time 3 / Location	Time 3 / Location
Antecedent	Antecedent	Antecedent	Antecedent	Antecedent
Consequence	Consequence	Consequence	Consequence	Consequence
Time 4 / Location	Time 4 / Location	Time 4 / Location	Time 4 / Location	Time 4 / Location
Antecedent	Antecedent	Antecedent	Antecedent	Antecedent
Consequence	Consequence	Consequence	Consequence	Consequence

Tracking Multiple Behaviors Example

Child's Name *Danny W.*   Date *3/19*

Behavior *Biting Self*		Behavior *Biting Others*		Behavior *Scratching Others*		Behavior *Hitting Others*		Behavior	
Time 1 9:35	Location *circle time*	Time 1 10:05	Location *block center*	Time 1 10:50	Location *in line*	Time 1 11:15	Location *snack table*	Time 1	Location
Antecedent ?		Antecedent *wanted adult to sit by him*		Antecedent *another student was talking to him*		Antecedent *another student bumped his arm*		Antecedent	
Consequence *5 min. time-out*		Consequence *redirected*		Consequence *time-out*		Consequence *apology/moved to another chair*		Consequence	
Time 2	Location	Time 2 10:15	Location *house center*	Time 2	Location	Time 2	Location	Time 2	Location
Antecedent		Antecedent *friend had doll he wanted*		Antecedent		Antecedent		Antecedent	
Consequence		Consequence *redirected*		Consequence		Consequence		Consequence	
Time 3	Location	Time 3	Location	Time 3	Location	Time 3	Location	Time 3	Location
Antecedent		Antecedent		Antecedent		Antecedent		Antecedent	
Consequence		Consequence		Consequence		Consequence		Consequence	
Time 4	Location	Time 4	Location	Time 4	Location	Time 4	Location	Time 4	Location
Antecedent		Antecedent		Antecedent		Antecedent		Antecedent	
Consequence		Consequence		Consequence		Consequence		Consequence	

Initial Behavior Analysis*

Child's Name _________________________   Date _____________________________

Setting ______________________________   Activity __________________________

Name of Person Completing Form ____

What happened just before the behavior occurred? ___________________________

____

____

Describe the behavior. ____

____

____

What was the consequence of the behavior? _________________________________

____

____

Date/Time	Location	No. of Occurrences	Consequences

Comments: ____

* This form can be used for observing the same behavior several times in one day or for observation over several days.

Initial Behavior Analysis Example

Child's Name   *Cindy B.*   Date   *3/15 – 3/19*

Setting   *kindergarten classroom*   Activity   *story time*

Name of Person Completing Form

What happened just before the behavior occurred?   *children sat on floor to hear*

teacher read story

Describe the behavior.   *repeatedly fell backward onto other children*

What was the consequence of the behavior?   *removed to sit in chair at desk during*

story after several requests to stop

Date/Time	Location	No. of Occurrences	Consequences
3/15	book center	/ / /	redirected 2x, moved to chair
3/16	book center	/ / / /	redirected 3x, moved to chair
3/17	book center	/ / /	redirected 2x, moved to chair
3/18	book center	/ / /	redirected 2x, moved to chair**
3/19	book center	/ /	redirected 1x, moved to chair

Comments: *** 3/18 – After being put in chair, she screamed and was removed to hallway.*

* This form can be used for observing the same behavior several times in one day or for observation over several days.

Record of Progress

Child's Name _______________________________________

Behavior _______________________________________

Social Skill Lesson _______________________________

Date Social Skill Lesson Initiated ___________________

Intervention Chart

Baseline ___________ (average # of occurrences in one day from *Initial Behavior Analysis*)

	Lesson Read?		How often does the behavior occur?									
	Yes	No										
Day 1												
Day 2												
Day 3												
Day 4												
Day 5												
Day 6												
Day 7												
Day 8												
Day 9												
Day 10												

Comments: ____

____

____

____

Record of Progress Example

Child's Name ___*Cindy B.*___

Behavior ___*falling back on other children during story time*___

Social Skill Lesson ___*Falling on Friends (Behavior)*___

Date Social Skill Lesson Initiated ___*3/18*___

Intervention Chart

Baseline ___*3x/day*___ (average # of occurrences in one day from *Initial Behavior Analysis*)

	Lesson Read?			**How often does the behavior occur?**								
	Yes	No										
Day 1	X			0								
Day 2	X			0								
Day 3		X		✓	✓	✓						
Day 4	X			0								
Day 5	X			0								
Day 6	X			0								
Day 7		X		0								
Day 8												
Day 9												
Day 10												

Comments: ____

____

____

____

Child's Name _______________________________

Daily Routines

❏ Morning Routine
Date ______________

____

❏ Getting Dressed
Date ______________

____

❏ Wearing Different Clothes
Date ______________

____

❏ Mealtime: I Eat My Own Food
Date ______________

____

❏ Trying New Food
Date ______________

____

❏ Going to Bed
Date ______________

____

❏ Weekend Morning
Date ______________

____

❏ Cleaning My Room
Date ______________

____

❏ After-school Day-care
Date ______________

____

Self-Care

❏ Brushing Teeth
Date ______________

____

❏ Shampooing Hair
Date ______________

____

❏ Clipping Fingernails
Date ______________

____

❏ Bath Time
Date ______________

____

❏ Using the Toilet
Date ______________

____

❏ Taking Medicine
Date ______________

____

Appliances/Safety

❏ Answering Machine
Date ______________

____

❏ The Vacuum Cleaner
Date ______________

____

❏ Electrical Outlets
Date ______________

____

❏ Hot and Cold Water
Date ______________

____

❏ Hot Iron
Date ______________

____

Child's Name _______________________________

Appliances/Safety, *continued*

❑ Hot Stove
Date _______________

____

❑ The Microwave
Date _______________

____

❑ Wearing My Seat Belt
Date _______________

____

❑ Sitting in the Back Seat
Date _______________

____

Family Relations

❑ Getting Help
Date _______________

____

❑ Others Talking on the Phone
Date _______________

____

❑ Favorite TV Show
Date _______________

____

❑ Watching One TV
Date _______________

____

❑ Sharing the TV
Date _______________

____

❑ Sharing the Computer
Date _______________

____

❑ Pets
Date _______________

____

❑ People Go Away
Date _______________

____

❑ The Baby-sitter
Date _______________

____

Special Occasions

❑ Not Going on a Trip
Date _______________

____

❑ Staying Away from Home
Date _______________

____

❑ Time-out
Date _______________

____

❑ Sick Sibling Stays Home
Date _______________

____

❑ Having Company
Date _______________

____

❑ My Birthday
Date _______________

____

❑ The Sprinkler
Date _______________

____

<table>
<tr><td colspan="7"><h1>Tracking Form for Lessons – Group</h1></td><td><h2>Home</h2></td></tr>
</table>

	Names:					
Daily Routines						
Morning Routine						
Getting Dressed						
Wearing Different Clothes						
Mealtime: I Eat My Own Food						
Trying New Food						
Going to Bed						
Weekend Morning						
Cleaning My Room						
After-school Day-care						
Self-Care						
Brushing Teeth						
Shampooing Hair						
Clipping Fingernails						
Bath Time						
Using the Toilet						
Taking Medicine						
Appliances/Safety						
Answering Machine						
The Vacuum Cleaner						
Electrical Outlets						
Hot and Cold Water						
Hot Iron						
Hot Stove						
The Microwave						
Wearing My Seat Belt						
Sitting in the Back Seat						
Family Relations						
Getting Help						
Others Talking on the Phone						
Favorite TV Show						

Home

Names:						
Family Relations, *continued*						
Watching One TV						
Sharing the TV						
Sharing the Computer						
Pets						
People Go Away						
The Baby-sitter						
Special Occasions						
Not Going on a Trip						
Staying Away from Home						
Time-out						
Sick Sibling Stays Home						
Having Company						
My Birthday						
The Sprinkler						

Overview of Lessons

Getting Along

Social Interactions

Eating

My Body

Behavior*

School Behavior

Home Behavior

Hurting Self/Others

Home

Daily Routines

Self-Care

Appliances/Safety

Family Relations

Special Occasions

I = Instructional
B = Behavioral

* All lessons are behavioral.

School

Routine Activities

First Day of School I
Riding the Bus to School I
Saying the Pledge of Allegiance I
Using a Schedule I
Using a Work Table I
I Finish My Work I
Listening to My Teacher Read a Story I
Listening to Friends Read Books I
Recess I
Cafeteria: Choosing Food . . . . I/B
Cafeteria: Carrying My Tray I
Cafeteria: I Eat My Own Food . . . . B
Cafeteria: Waiting with Friends . . . . B
Nap Time I
Using Math Manipulatives . . . . I/B
Using Markers . . . . I/B
Using the Computer . . . . I/B
Cleaning Up the Room . . . . I/B

Extra-Curricular Activities

Transitions I
Gym Class I
Going to Speech I
Library I

Social Skills

Quiet Voice . . . . I/B
Raising My Hand . . . . I/B
Waiting for Help . . . . I/B
Walking in Line . . . . I/B

Special Days

Going to an Event I
Field Trip I
Somebody Different Picks Me Up I
Holidays Away from School I
My Teacher Is Sick I
Fire Drill I
Tornado Drill I

Self-Care

Dirty Hands I
Washing Hands I
Using the Rest Room I
Covering My Cough and Sneeze I
Wearing a Helmet I
Going to the School Nurse I
Getting My Temperature Taken I

Community*

Community Services

The Haircut
The Dentist
A Cavity
The Check-up
Immunizations
Shopping
The Car Wash
The Post Office
New Shoes
New Clothes
The Library: Choosing Books
The Library: Story Time
The Video Store
The Restaurant
Fast Food
Drive-Thru Food

Social Activities

Visiting a Friend's House
The Birthday Party
The Movie Theater
The Skating Rink
The Swimming Pool
The Zoo
The Park
The Picnic
Taking a Vacation
Camping
Fishing
Soccer Practice
The Soccer Game
The T-Ball Game
The Parade
The Clown
Fireworks

Transportation

The Airplane
The Boat Ride
The Bus Ride
The Elevator
The Escalator

Safety

Crossing the Street
I Can't Find My Parent

I = Instructional
B = Behavioral

* All lessons are instructional.

References and Resources

Frith, U. *Autism: Explaining the Enigma.* Oxford, England: Blackwell, 1989.

Grandin, T. *Thinking in Pictures.* New York: Doubleday, 1995.

Gray, C. (ed.). *The Morning News.* Newsletter available by subscription through Jenison Public Schools, Jenison, MI. (To order, call 616-457-8955.)

Gray, C. *The New Social Story Book.* Arlington, TX: Future Horizons, 1994.

Harrington, K. *For Parents and Professionals: Autism.* E. Moline, IL: LinguiSystems, Inc., 1998.

Hodgdon, L.A. *Visual Strategies for Improving Communication. Volume 1: Practical Supports for School and Home.* Troy, MI: Quirk Roberts Publishing, 1995.

Koski, P.S. *Autism & PDD: Picture Stories and Language Activities.* E. Moline, IL: LinguiSystems, Inc., 1998.

Mayer-Johnson, R. *Boardmaker* Software. Salona Beach, CA: Mayer-Johnson, 1995.

Richard, G.J. *The Source for Autism.* E. Moline, IL: LinguiSystems, Inc., 1997.

Rollins, P., Wambacq, I., Dowell, D., Mathews, L., and Reese, P. "An Intervention Technique for Children with Autistic Spectrum Disorder: Joint Attention Routines." *Journal of Communication Disorders*, Vol. 31, 1998, pp. 181-193.

1-00-9876543